# Alphabet Affirmations For Girls of Color

**This Book Belongs To:**

_____

Life Chronicles Publishing

ISBN- 978-1-950649-73-0

Illustrator: Hajra Mazhar

Cover Design: Life Chronicles Publishing

Life Chronicles Publishing Copyright © 2019

lifechroniclespublishing.com

All rights reserved. No part of this book may be reproduced in any form or by any electronic or mechanical means, including information storage and retrieval systems, with or without permission from the publisher or author, except in the case of a reviewer, who may quote brief passages embodied in critical articles or in a review.

To my village,
Thank you. ❤

# A
I am athletic, aware, and awesome.

# B
I am brave, bold, and beautiful.

# C
I am courageous, creative, and confident.

## D
I am diligent, driven, and dynamic.

## E
I am empathetic, empowered, and enough.

## F
I am fearless, funny, and fantastic.

# G

I am gifted, gracious, and generous.

# H

I am honest, humorous, and humble.

# I

I am intelligent, independent, and inspired.

**J**

I am joyful, jazzy, and just.

**K**

I am kind, keen, and knowledgeable.

**L**

I am limitless, lively, and loved.

I am mindful, marvelous, and magical.

I am nifty, noble, and nurturing.

I am observant, optimistic, and open-minded.

# P

I am proud, peaceful, and positive.

# Q

I am quick-thinking and I am a queen.

# R

I am respectful, responsible
and I do what is right.

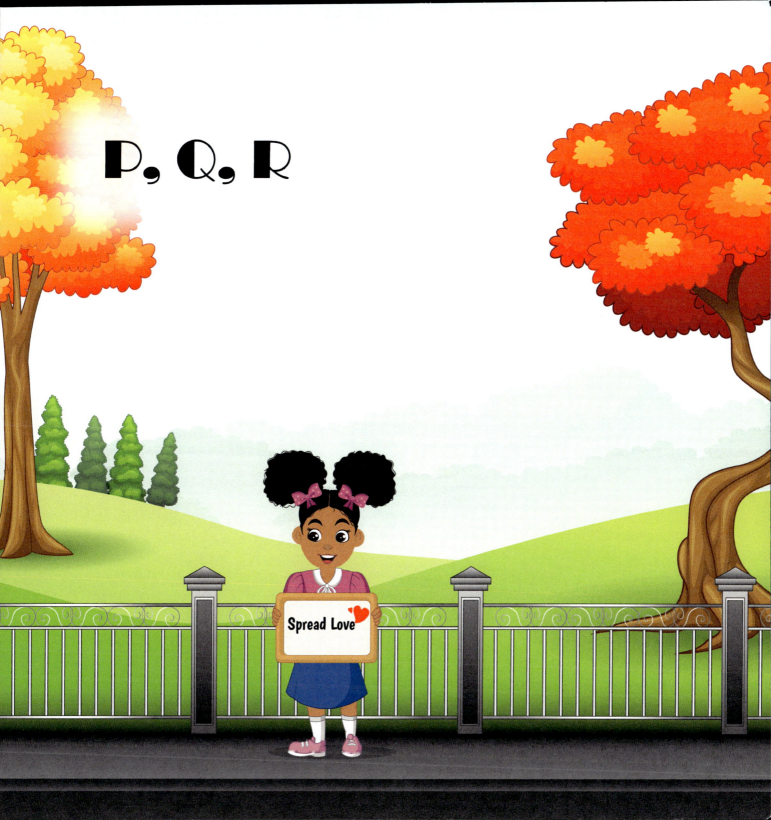

**S**
I am strong, selfless, and savvy.

**T**
I am tenacious, talented, and thankful.

**U**
I am unique, understanding,
and upbeat.

I am vibrant, vivid, and valued.

I am worthy, wise, and warm-hearted.

I am eXceptional and I will eXcel.

## Y

I am youthful and yippee! I love me.

## Z

I am zestful, zippy, and zen.

Made in the USA
Middletown, DE
05 May 2022